The Mystery Of The Three Worlds

Manly P. Hall

Kessinger Publishing's Rare Reprints

Thousands of Scarce and Hard-to-Find Books on These and other Subjects!

- Americana
- Ancient Mysteries
- Animals
- Anthropology
- Architecture
- Arts
- Astrology
- Bibliographies
- Biographies & Memoirs
- Body, Mind & Spirit
- Business & Investing
- Children & Young Adult
- Collectibles
- Comparative Religions
- Crafts & Hobbies
- Earth Sciences
- Education
- Ephemera
- Fiction
- Folklore
- Geography
- Health & Diet
- History
- Hobbies & Leisure
- Humor
- Illustrated Books
- Language & Culture
- Law
- Life Sciences
- Literature
- Medicine & Pharmacy
- Metaphysical
- Music
- Mystery & Crime
- Mythology
- Natural History
- Outdoor & Nature
- Philosophy
- Poetry
- Political Science
- Science
- Psychiatry & Psychology
- Reference
- Religion & Spiritualism
- Rhetoric
- Sacred Books
- Science Fiction
- Science & Technology
- Self-Help
- Social Sciences
- Symbolism
- Theatre & Drama
- Theology
- Travel & Explorations
- War & Military
- Women
- Yoga
- *Plus Much More!*

We kindly invite you to view our catalog list at:
http://www.kessinger.net

THIS ARTICLE WAS EXTRACTED FROM THE BOOK:

Man the Grand Symbol of the Mysteries

BY THIS AUTHOR:

Manly P. Hall

ISBN 1417949856

READ MORE ABOUT THE BOOK AT OUR WEB SITE:

http://www.kessinger.net

OR ORDER THE COMPLETE
BOOK FROM YOUR FAVORITE STORE

ISBN 1417949856

THE MYSTERY OF THE THREE WORLDS

CHAPTER III

IN accordance with the doctrines which had descended to them from their divine instructors, initiated priests of an older world regarded man as an epitome of the whole universal order and, therefore, a textbook of all mysteries, earthly and divine. Anatomy and physiology were cultivated as divine sciences and studied not for themselves alone but as aspects of sacred learning and keys to the heavenly arcanum. Benedictus Figulus writes that of the three books "from which I may learn very wisdom," the second "is the Small Book, which with all its leaves and pieces is taken from the larger work. This is man himself." In developing their concept of the relationship between the superior and the inferior orders of existence, the Cabalists denominated the ruler of the Macrocosm, *Macroprosophus,* "the Vast Countenance," and the ruler of the microcosm, *Microprosophus,* "the Lesser Countenance." According to at least one interpretation, "the Great Face" is God and "the Little Face," man—one the Supreme Agent, the other the miniature of that Agent; Deity enthroned in the divine sphere and man in the natural. "On man God stamped his seal and sign of his power, on him he has imprinted his own image and superscription, his arms and his portraiture. *Dixit Deus, faciamus hominem ad imaginem nostram, secundum similitudinem nostram.* * * * Hence he is called the microcosm, or little world, the recapitulation of all things, the ligament of angels and beasts, heavenly and earthly, spiritual and corporeal, the perfection of the whole work, the honour and miracle of nature." (Culpeper in *The Family Physician.*)

Blinded by its own diversified achievements, the present generation is prone to underestimate the knowledge of anatomy and other sciences posessed by older civilizations. The ravages of time and the vandalism of man have obliterated most of the records of such ancient learning. Enough remains, however, to convince the open-minded that at some remote period there existed upon this planet a race of supermen who carved their wisdom into the face of mountains and marked the broad surface of earth with pyramids and other monuments. Professor James H. Breasted, of the University of Chicago, one of the greatest living Egyptologists, has recently translated a papyrus written seventeen centuries B. C. and presumably copied from an original still older by a thousand years. "For the first time recorded in human speech," he says, "our treatise contains the word 'brain,' which is unknown in any other language of this age, or any other treatise of the third millenium B. C. The earliest discussions of the brain have hitherto been found in Greek medical documents probably over two thousand years later than our Egyptian treatise." There is also evidence in the document that at least one old Egyptian understood the localization of brain control of muscles. (See the commentaries by Professor Breasted upon the Edwin Smith Surgical Papyrus.) With every passing day, it becomes more evident that the priest-physicians of the elder world acquired an amazing knowledge of certain occult or hidden processes continually going on in the human body, as yet unrecognized by the savants of our enlightened (?) age.

In his *Secret Societies of all Ages,* Charles Heckethorne describes the human figure set up in the sanctuaries of the learned not as an object for idolatrous worship but as a constant reminder of the harmonies and proportions of the world. Pythagoras declared that the Universal Creator had fashioned two bodies in His own image: The first was Cosmos, with its myriads of suns, moons, and planets; the second was man, in whose internal parts was reflected the entire universe, so that as Boehme has said, the human constitution bears the stamp or seal or signature of the whole mundane order. For this reason, the priests of the primitive tradition, in order to facilitate their study of the natural sciences, caused the statue of the Grand Man to be set up in the midst of the Holy Place to symbolize the divine power in all its intricate manifestations. This mysterious figure—the symbolic Adam or pattern of the species which stood above the primitive altars—was like certain similar figures found in some old books and occasionally met with in the Orient even today; that is, it was in the nature of a manikin and, like the emblematic hands found in the ruins of Roman cities, was covered with hieroglyphics either carved upon its surface or painted thereon with non-fading pigments. The statue may even have opened, revealing the relative positions of the organs, bones, muscles, nerves, and other parts. Possibly the interior revealed the orbits of the planets, etc. One cannot but recall the Hermetic figure of Isis, her body covered with curious hieroglyphics and her belt studded with stars; or the Diana of Ephesus, bearing upon her parts the undeciphered words, *Aski-kataski-haix-tetrax-damnameneus-aision,* which, according to Hesychius, were engraved upon her belt or zone (See *Œdipus Ægyptiacus,* by Athanasius Kircher); or, again, the Sophia of the Gnostic vision, upon whose figure shone out in regular arrangement the letters of the Greek alphabet.

Gradually through ages of research the initiates of the various Mystery Schools contributed a mass of details to the fundamental principles set forth by the first philosophers, and by the time Egypt had reached the crowning glory of her civilization the manikin of the microcosm was a mass of intricate hieroglyphics and symbolic figures, each with a secret meaning reserved for the elect. The measurements of the symbolic man were a basic standard by which it was possible to measure by estimation and proportion every part of Cosmos. In its most perfect form, the manikin was a glorious composite emblem, witness to a knowledge possessed by the sages and hierophants of Isis, Osiris, and Serapis, and which by the Egyptians was communicated to the Greeks and other nations. The Grand Man seen by Nebuchadnezzar in his dream, with its golden head and feet of clay, as well as the mysterious figure which walked amidst the candlesticks of *Revelation* refer unquestionably to this Universal Adam, this heroic epitome of all things. In an oracle delivered to the King of Cyprus, Serapis describes himself as the Universal Man in these words:

"A god I am such as I show to thee,
The Starry Heavens are my head, my trunk the sea,
Earth forms my feet, mine ears the air supplies,
The Sun's far-darting, brilliant rays, mine eyes."

Those initiated into the Mysteries became themselves, in turn, embodiments of the sacred truths. So we learn that those accepted into the Mithraic Rites were invested with loose tunics or capes on which, according to Maurice, in his

Indian Antiquites, were depicted the celestial constellations, each with its zone or belt containing a representation of the figures of the zodiac. Like the starry hat which the gods bestowed upon Atys, these cloaks strewn with stars and constellations signified the new and heavenly body which the gods conferred upon the wise. The corporeal nature was transmuted by the Mysteries into a celestial nature, and men who had previously enveloped themselves in the dark raiment of form, having been "raised" into the presence of the immortals, put on a new and luminous garb resplendent with the heavenly lights. This is the same cloak to which Apuleius refers when he says that men devoted to the service of Divinity speak of it as the "Olympic garment."

In some old temple before an ancient altar long since crumbled away, but which then supported the radiant "philosophic manikin"—the very embodiment of wisdom—Hermes may have stood when he addressed the following words to his son, Tatian: "If thou wouldst contemplate the Creator even in perishable things, in things which are on the earth, or in the deep, reflect, O my son, on the formation of man in his mother's womb; contemplate the skill of the Workman; learn to know Him according to the divine beauty of the work. Who formed the orb of the eye? Who pierced the openings of the nostrils and of the ears? Who made the mouth to open? Who traced out the channels of the veins? Who made the bones hard? Who covered the flesh with skin? Who separated the fingers and the toes? Who made the feet broad? Who hollowed out the pores? Who spread out the spleen? Who formed the heart like a pyramid? Who made the sides wide? Who formed the caverns of the lungs? Who made the honorable parts of the body conspicuous and concealed the others? * * * Who made all these things? Who is the mother, who is the father, if it be not the only and invisible God who has created all things by His will?"

Then came the age of idolatry. The Mysteries decayed from within. The profane sat in the seats of wisdom. Wars destroyed the old orders. The light was swallowed up in darkness. The life departed and only the empty forms remained. None could be found to translate those symbols and emblems which constituted the secret language of the initiates. The identity of the manikin which stood over the altar was lost. It was only remembered that the figure was a sacred thing and had been revered by earlier ages as a glorious symbol of universal power. The "textbook of the philosophers" came to be looked upon as a god, even as the very god in whose image man had been made. The secret knowledge of the purpose for which the manikin had been constructed having been lost beyond recovery, the degenerate priestcrafts worshipped the actual wood and stone until finally the common lack of understanding brought down the temples in ruins and the statues crumbled away with the civilizations that had forgotten their meanings.

If we would be truly wise, we must be correctly informed as to the will of the Creative Agent as this will is manifested through the infinite diversity of creation. "The investigation of the use of the parts of the body," wrote the great Galen, "lays the foundation of a truly scientific theology which is much greater and more precious than all medicine." It was from the Hermetic premise set forth by the immortal Trismegistus upon the Smaragdine Tablet—"the inferior agrees with the superior and the superior with the inferior"—that the initiates of the old Mysteries established the science of correspondences. (See Swedenborg.) "Gnothi Seauthon" (Know thyself) was inscribed over the portals of the Secret House that those called to sacred matters might by pondering upon these words be fully informed as to the beginning of wisdom. Moving upon the Paracelsian premise that "visible forms are merely external expressions of invisible principles," it is possible through meditation upon the harmony of bodily form and function to discover those laws of life by which the symphony of being is maintained. Pythagoras places the instrument of wisdom in the hands of every man when he is made to say in *The New Pearl of Great Price* that "man is the measure of all things."

How can man in the smallness of his consciousness express a more glorious conception of the creative plan than through such a vision as Eliphas Levi gives us in his *History of Magic?* "That synthesis of the word," writes the great Cabalist, "formulated by the human figure, ascended slowly and emerged from the water, like the sun in its rising. When the eyes appeared, light was made; when the mouth was manifested, there was the creation of spirits and the word passed into expression. The entire head was revealed, and this completed the first day of creation. The shoulders, the arms, the breast arose, and thereupon work began. With one hand the Divine Image put back the sea, while with the other it raised up continents and mountains. The Image grew and grew; the generative organs appeared, and all beings began to increase and multiply. The form stood at length erect, having one foot upon the earth and one upon the waters. Beholding itself at full length in the ocean of creation, it breathed on its own reflection and called its likeness into life. It said: Let us make man—and thus man was made. There is nothing so beautiful in the masterpiece of any poet as this vision of creation accomplished by the prototype of humanity. Hereby is man but the shadow of a shadow, and yet he is the image of divine power. He can also stretch forth his hands from East to West; to him is the earth given as a dominion. Such is Adam Kadmon, the primordial Adam of the Kaballists. Such is the sense in which he is depicted as a giant; and this is why Swedenborg, haunted in his dreams by reminiscences of the

—From Myer's Qabbalah.

A FIGURE OF THE MICROCOSM SHOWING THE SEATS OF THE TRINITY OF MAN

Kabalah, says that entire creation is only a titanic man and that we are made in the image of the universe."

In *The Divine Pymander* it is written that Nature, having been embraced by the Man (the Protogonas, who contained within himself the concord of the seven fiery and spiritual Governors), brought forth seven men in correspondence with the nature of the sidereal seven, and these seven men were male-female and moved in the air. They apparently correspond with the Kumaras, the virgin youths of the Vedas. They were the progenitors of the races and their origin was "the mystery kept hid until this day." (See *The Thrice Greatest Hermes*.) At this point we wish to establish certain arbitrary definitions for the words *androgyne* and *hermaphrodite*. Though generally regarded as synonymous, we would like to establish a fine point of difference between the terms. The word *androgyne* will be used to represent the equilibrium of the sexual potentialities in the soul, a state natural to the divine man. On the other hand, the word *hermaphrodite* is to be limited strictly to the phenomenon of incomplete sexual determination in the physical body.

The first man of the Judaistic system was created male-female, in the image of the Logoi, or the Elohim. He was the Celestial Androgyne, in whose likeness the second man (i.e., the terrestrial Adam) was formed. The lesser Adam in his terrestrial state was also androgynous, for he was an "air" or "sky" man—that is, he had not as yet become involved in material evolution. Only after Eve was taken out of him did he lose his divine completeness—that is, the one became two and the creative agent was distinguished as both agent and patient, or male and female. In *The Zohar* it is stated that "Adam was created with two faces," and in another place, "And the Lord, blessed be He, parted him, and made two." Most ancient nations have legendary accounts of androgynous beings who existed at a remote time and were the progenitors of present humanity. These beings were metaphysical, however, possesed extraordinary powers, and were in all respects *superior* to mankind. Were these semi-divine creatures but mythological monsters of the imagination, or did they actually exist in the first ages only to vanish away like the mysterious Kings of Edom?

If life, the moulder of all form, is innately androgynous, we shall not be surprised to discover that the first physical bodies with which life invested itself bear evidence of this completeness. "All the invertebrate ancestors of man," writes Ernst Haeckel, "from the Gastraeda up to the Chordonia, must have been hermaphrodite. So, probably were the earliest skulled animals. One extremely weighty piece of evidence of this is afforded by the remarkable fact, that even in Vertebrates, in Man as well as other Vertebrates, the original rudiment of the sexual organs is hermaphrodite." (See *The Evolution of Man*.) Were the older writers, then, wiser and of greater vision than those who, coming after, ridiculed their words? Is the story of Adam and Eve a faithful narrative of evolutionary progress, setting forth what Haeckel would have called "the separation of the sexes," which took place in the "secondary" or "farther course of tribal history"? How many scientific mysteries are concealed under the religious and philosophic writings of classical and non-classical antiquity? What of the unnumbered specters of various forms, centaurs and double shapes which confronted Æneas at the gates of hell? What of the "one-eyed" men, the "winged" men, and the "hundred-armed" Briareus? Are the accounts of the "giants" and the "scorpion" men and the men with the "bodies of serpents" devoid of reason, or did they faithfully picture under figures and allegories facts in the genesis of form no more amazing than those now generally admitted by men of letters?

There is substance for thought in the fables of the ancients. Witness the "dragon" mines of the Chinese, where the teeth of prehistoric monsters are still excavated for medicinal purposes. The dragons which figure in the legends of Cathay most certainly existed, only sicence knows them under other names. They were the huge animals of another world and,

—From *Amphitheatrum Sapientae Aeternae*.

THE PHILOSOPHICAL ANDROGYNE ACCORDING TO
HEINRICH KHUNRATH

From the union of the sun and moon arises the bird Azoth, with its peacock tail. The bird symbolizes both the Philosopher's Stone and the soul.

were their bones not irrefutable testimony, would have been denied by this age as the chimeras of a fevered dream. Plato declared that male and female are but the halves of a primitive androgyne which once existed as a separate type but was afterwards divided into kinds and thus lost its identity in its progeny. Of this undivided type he writes: "The Androgynes, for so they were called, had not only the male and female faces, but also possessed the sexual distinctions of both. Of these creatures, likewise, nothing now exists but the *name,* which survives as a *stigma,* and which is considered *infamous.*" When Plato says that nothing remains of the androgynes but the name, he clearly indicates that this primitive creation is not to be confused with the hermaphrodites and intermediate types which most certainly existed in his day. Plato then goes on to explain the origin of the three kinds of beings, saying "that the males were formed by the *Sun;* the females by the *Earth;* and the mixed race of Androgynes by the *Moon:* —which partakes both of the *Sun* and the *Earth.*" (See *The Rosicrucians,* by Hargrave Jennings.)

Here Plato is concealing a mystery as he did in his account of Atlantis. The sun which formed the males is the symbol of spirit and also of the gods or divinities who move through the agency of the solar power. The earth which formed the females is the symbol of matter and of mankind, the negative creation, the matrix, etc. The moon which formed the androgynes, as "partaking of both," represents the soul, or mind, the spiritual androgyne, the middle race, the "heroes" or demigods, who partake of both qualities, and again of the initiates, the self-born, of whom the androgynous phoenix is the esoteric symbol. The intellect as the link between superiors and inferiors is in equilibrium and, being balanced, unites the virtues of both extremities. "The truth is," writes Coleridge, "a great mind must be androgynous." The soul is the first androgynous being to precipitate body out of itself without recourse to any other creature. As soul equilibrates itself in the body which it has precipitated, the mystery of the Melchizedek will be revealed. According to *The Secret Doctrine,* humanity will, in the course of countless ages, again become male-female, achieving through evolution the potential equilibrium which has been within it since the beginning. The sympathetic nervous system (the soul ganglia) will gradually increase in significance and unite into a true spinal cord, so that man will have two complete parallel spinal systems. When this point has been reached, man will be negatively androgynous or philosophically hermaphroditic—that is, he will be both sexes in one, each pole, however, manifesting through its own organism or bodily system.

Writing in the thirteenth century, Amaury de Chartres, held among what Hargrave Jennings terms "other fanciful notions" that at the end of the world both sexes would be reunited in the same person. This is in agreement with the ancient philosophical teachings that as man's human evolution approaches its end the cerebrospinal and sympathetic nervous systems will gradually draw together and ultimately "merge" into one. Soul will then be unified in body, resulting in what may be termed the ultimate type—the true androgyne, the man who is fashioned like his Father in heaven. In harmony with this doctrine, the ancient alchemists symbolized spiritual achievement by a two-headed bi-sexual figure. The androgynous Ishwara, is pictured by Inman in his *Ancient Faiths* as having the right half of his body male and the left half female, and as the first man is the archetype of the human race in both its primitive and ultimate states. The Mystery gods, such as Serapis and Dionysius, are usually shown heavily robed to conceal the fact that while they have the bearded faces of men, their bodies combine male and female attributes. The Templars were accused of worshipping the androgynous

Baphomet, and the bearded Venus was an object of veneration among the initiated Greeks and Latins.

Under the heading, "Hints on the Future," Madame Blavatsky writes: "As time passes on there will be more and more ether in the air. When ether fills the air, then will be born children without fathers. In Virginia there is an apple tree of a special kind. It does not blossom but bears fruit from a kind of berry without any seeds. This will gradually extend to animals and then to men. Women will bear children without impregnation, and in the Seventh Round there will appear men who can reproduce themselves. In the Seventh Race of the Fourth Round, men will change their skins every year and will have new toe and finger nails. People will become more psychic, then spiritual. Last of all in the Seventh Round, Buddhas will be born without sin." (See Vol. III, *The Secret Doctrine*.) The spiritul nature is neither male nor female, but both in perfect balance—the Ego is an androgynous entity. Hence, its perfect manifestation must be through an androgynous self-generating body, but ages must pass before the human race can sufficiently master the secrets of universal polarity for every man to become a complete entity in himself. Understanding is only possible when the positive and negative potentialities are in equilibrium; neither the male nor the female can be perfect of itself. Such is the mystery of the Priest-King Melchizedek, Prince of Salem, who was his own father and his own mother, and in whose footsteps all initiates of the Mysteries must follow if they would be priests forever after the Order of Melchizedek.

Interpreting the Orphic tradition, the Pythagorean initiates divided the universe into three parts, termed the *Supreme,* the *superior,* and the *inferior* worlds. From John Reuchlin's *Explication of the Pythagoric Doctrine,* we learn that the

Supreme world (which contains all the others and which consists of a single divine essence) is called that of Deity, and, being without beginning or end, is the eternal abode of existence, substance, essence, and Nature. The superior world (which "shineth" with incorporeal natures) is called that of the supermundane powers, the divine examplars and the "seals of the world." In it dwell also those divinities which, though of divine origin, are somewhat removed from First Cause and partake to a degree of natural substance. Here, too, reside those "heroes" who, though sons of the earth, have achieved to the state of demigod-hood by reason of transcendent virtues or accomplishments. The inferior world (which is the least of the three and is contained within both the others) is called that of the angels, gods, and demons. Here abide "bodies and magnitudes with their appropriate Intelligences, the Movers of the spheres, the Overseers and guardians of things generate and corruptible, and such as are assigned to take care of bodies." (See *De Mysteriis Pythagoricis.*) In general, the inferior world corresponded with the physical universe, or mundane sphere, the home of mortal spirits or, possibly more correctly, the temporary domicile of spirits in the state of mortality. In addition to such beings, who are the "mankind" of the philosophers, the inferior universe included the three lower kingdoms of Nature: the mineral, plant, and animal; also the subterreous elemental deities and tutelary spirits. It was this concept of the universal order that moved Aristotle to the comment: "The Pythagoreans affirm that the whole and all things are terminated by three."

From these doctrines of the enlightened pagans the Fathers of the primitive Christian Church derived their opinions concerning the departments of cosmos. The creation, they declared, subsists in three departments, of which the first is heaven, the second earth, and the third hell. The three crowns of the papal tiara signify the sovereignty of the Apostolic Church over the spiritual, temporal, and purgatorial spheres—the tripartite universe of the Orphic cosmologists. To the early Christian, the spiritual sphere was the abode of the Godhead in its triple aspect. The temporal sphere was

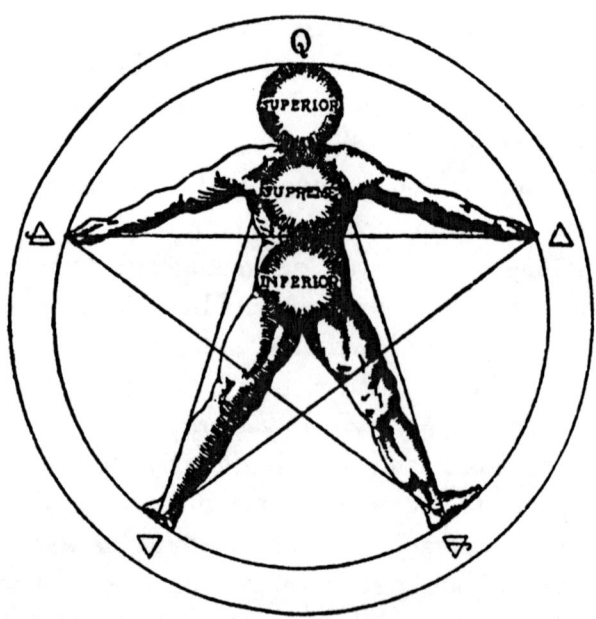

THE PYTHAGOREAN PENTALPHA WITH THE PARTS OF THE WORLD ASSIGNED TO THE THREE MAJOR BODILY CAVITIES

originally the abode of the "hierarchies" and "saints" (the latter the "heroes" of the Greeks—the mortal immortals and the immortal mortals). Later the temporal sphere was identified with the world of mankind in general. The purgatorial sphere was originally the "sublunary estate," the abode of mortals (the Tartarus of the classical philosophers), but later the Church defined it as the posthumous state or condition of the soul after the death of the body, a condition in which sins were expiated, etc. Those informed upon such subjects realized heaven, earth, and hell to be qualities or conditions of being by which the One Life expressed itself through phases or aspects. Of these the three primary phases are Consciousness, Intelligence, and Force—the "Three Witnesses," the Trinity in Unity, and "the One in essence and Three in aspect" of the Hermetic Emerald. The three faces of the Deity are, therefore, the three worlds Plutarch so beautifully sets forth in his explanation of the Forty-seventh Problem of Euclid. By Consciousness the heavens were established; by Force the earth was lifted up from the deep and set upon its eternal foundations; and by Intelligence (the Homeric chain) heaven and earth were bound together—the Ark, the Anchor, and the Cable-Tow.

Applied to man generally, the three worlds correspond with the three major divisions of his composite nature—spirit, soul (or mind), and body. In his physical constitution, they have their analogy in the three major cavities of the body—the spirit to the thoracic, the soul (or mind) to the cranial, and the body to the abdominal. These are the three main chambers of the Pyramid and also the symbolic rooms in which are given the Entered Apprentice, Fellowcraft, and Master Mason's degrees in modern Freemasonry. Each of these three bodily cavities is, in turn, regarded as divisible into three parts, and all these together constitute nine, and finally enclosed within the greater cavity of the auric egg, produce the perfect human decad, or ten. Of these bodily cavities and their significance, Eliphas Levi hints in his *Transcendental Magic*: "Whatsoever is in the great world is reproduced in the small. Hence, we have three centers [analogous to the cavities of the classical writers] of fluidic attraction and projection—the brain, the heart, or epigastric region, and the genital organ." The Trinity in man, therefore, was believed to reside in the three great cavities of the body: Brahma in the heart, Vishnu in the brain, and Shiva (whose appropriate symbol is the *lingam*) in the generative system. Each of these deities has a threefold manifestation—the crea-

—From Collectio Operum.

A FIGURE FROM THE ROSICRUCIAN WRITINGS OF ROBERT FLUDD, PORTRAYING THE ELEMENTAL WORLD IN ITS PRIMARY STATE— THE CHAOS OF THE ELEMENTS.

tive, preservative, and disintegrative aspects. These phases, in turn, were enthroned in lesser cavities contained within the greater ones. A good example of the secondary divisions of these major cavities will be found in the remarks concerning the doctrines of the Arabians in the section on the ventricles of the brain, in Chapter X.

In the correspondences between man and the three worlds, the heart came to be regarded as analogous to the heavens, the brain to the earth, and the generative system to hades, or the underworld. We learn from the Greeks that the awful caverns of Tartarus were under the very roots of Olympus

—From De Humanini Corporis Fabrica.

VESALIUS' DRAWING OF THE ABDOMINAL CAVITY AND ITS CONTENTS.

By comparing this figure with that of Fludd's on the opposite page, it will be evident that the elemental world of the Rosicrucian was depicted in the general form of the intestinal tract.

and that the purgatorial chambers of initiation in the ancient temples were always subterranean, representing by their place and arrangement the windings of the intestinal tract. "Man is the mirror of the universe," wrote van Helmont, "and his *triple* nature stands in relationship to all things." The importance of recognizing the analogies upon which the philosophy of the microcosm was built up may not be at first apparent. As the mind penetrates farther into the mystery, it will become evident, however, that the whole universe is suspended like a foetus from its triform cause, termed in the Mysteries *being, life,* and *intelligence*. By *being* is intimated that which is the unmoved support of all existence; by *life* that which is the self-moving origin of all activity; and by *intellect* that which is moved. As Proclus might have said, good is that which abides, wisdom is that which moves, and beauty is that which is moved, manifesting the impulses of the first order. "Like a foetus, he [man] is suspended, by all his three spirits, in the matrix of the Macrocosmos." (H. P. Blavatsky in *Isis Unveiled*.)

According to Pindar, the Pythagorean, the universe was an ensouled animal, and Plutarch adds that the sun is its heart, the moon its liver, etc. Hence, we find man referred to as the "little animal" by Galen, the "little world" or the "little heaven" by Philo, the "little diacosm" by Porphyry, and the "lesser world" by Solon. (See *Orpheus,* by G. R. S. Mead.) After dividing the body into its noble and ignoble parts according to Laurentius, Burton follows the ancient order by recognizing three regions or the threefold division of the whole body: the head containing the animal organs; the chest "in which the Heart as King keeps his court;" and the abdomen, "in which the Liver resides as a *Legat a latere*." Burton then invites his reader to enter into the contemplation of the mysteries of the body as though he had been brought into the presence of "some sacred Temple, or Majestical Palace, to behold not the matter only, but the singular Art, Workmanship, and counsel of this, our great Creator." Proclus correlates man to the world by saying that, like the universe, he has mind and reason, a divine body and a perishable body. Paracelsus adds the following testimony: "Whoever desires to be a practical philosopher ought to be able to indicate heaven and hell in the microcosm, and to find everything in man that exists in heaven and upon the earth."

In his analysis of the anatomy of the microcosm, Robert Fludd summarizes the opinions of earlier authorities by means of the curious figures reproduced herewith. In studying these diagrams, *one point particularly should be borne in mind.* The head as the highest part of the physical frame was used to represent the *empyrean,* or the highest part of the universe. The heart, however, is the noblest organ of the body and is, therefore, the true "head" in man and the actual source of all inspiration and truth. The cranium is but the outer bodily symbol of the heart. Thus, the highest part of the physical structure becomes analogous to the most spiritual organ, which is, therefore, actually the "highest" part of man. In the universe, Deity is presumed to dwell in the furthermost and uppermost parts, but the philosophers understand His true abode to be in the heart of man, than which there is no higher place. The entire problem is not one of literalism, but of soul qualities abiding in higher dimensional vistas.

In Fludd's first figure the human body is divided into three compartments by parallel arcs. The upper division is called *Coelum Empyreum* and is assigned to the head. The central division is called *Coelum Æthereum* and is assigned to the thoracic cavity. The lower division is called *Coelum Elementarium* and is assigned to the abdominal cavity. The heavenly world of the head is separated from the airy, or ethereal, world of the chest by the double line running

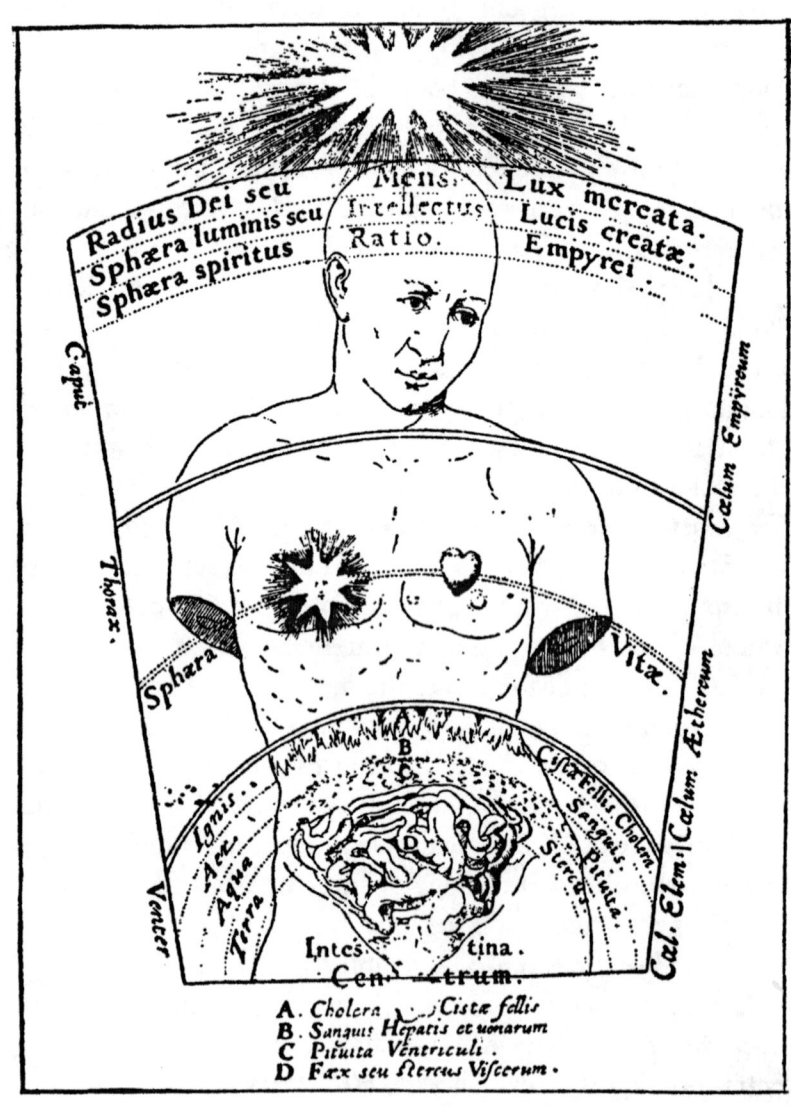

—From Collectio Operum.

FLUDD'S KEY TO UNIVERSAL ANATOMY.

The Cabalistic Adam as the first man and archetype of humanity.

through the shoulders. Fludd's interpretation of the three departments of the head will be found at the beginning of the section on the ventricles of the brain. The central, or thoracic, cavity is separated into a superior and an inferior half of the orbit of the sun (called *Sphæra Vitæ,* "the sphere of life"), which is shown as moving on a plane with the human heart. This division of the chest is in harmony with Plato's dissertation on this subject in *The Timæus,* where he says: "And fearing to pollute the divine element, they gave the mortal soul a separate habitation in the breast, parted off from the head by a narrow isthmus. And as in a house the women's apartments are divided from the men's, the cavity of the thorax was divided into two parts, a higher and a lower. The higher of the two, which is the seat of courage and anger, lies nearer to the head, between the midriff and the neck, and assists reason in restraining the desires. The heart is the house of guard in which all veins meet and through them reason sends her commands to the extremity of her kingdom. * * * The part of the soul which desires meat and drink was placed between the midriff and navel, where they made a sort of manger; and here they bound it down, like a wild animal, away from the council-chamber, leaving the better principle undisturbed to advise quietly for the good of the whole."

Although not depicted herein, the three superior planets (Saturn, Jupiter, and Mars) and the three inferior planets (Venus, Mercury, and the Moon) should be regarded as moving in this region of the ethereal, or thoracic, heaven. By their position upon the body they would signify the vital organs distributed within the thorax and clustered about the sovereign sun (the heart). The orbit of the sun corresponds in general with the location of the diaphragm, Plato's "midriff," a muscle frequently used in mediaeval symbolism to

82   Man—The Grand Symbol of the Mysteries

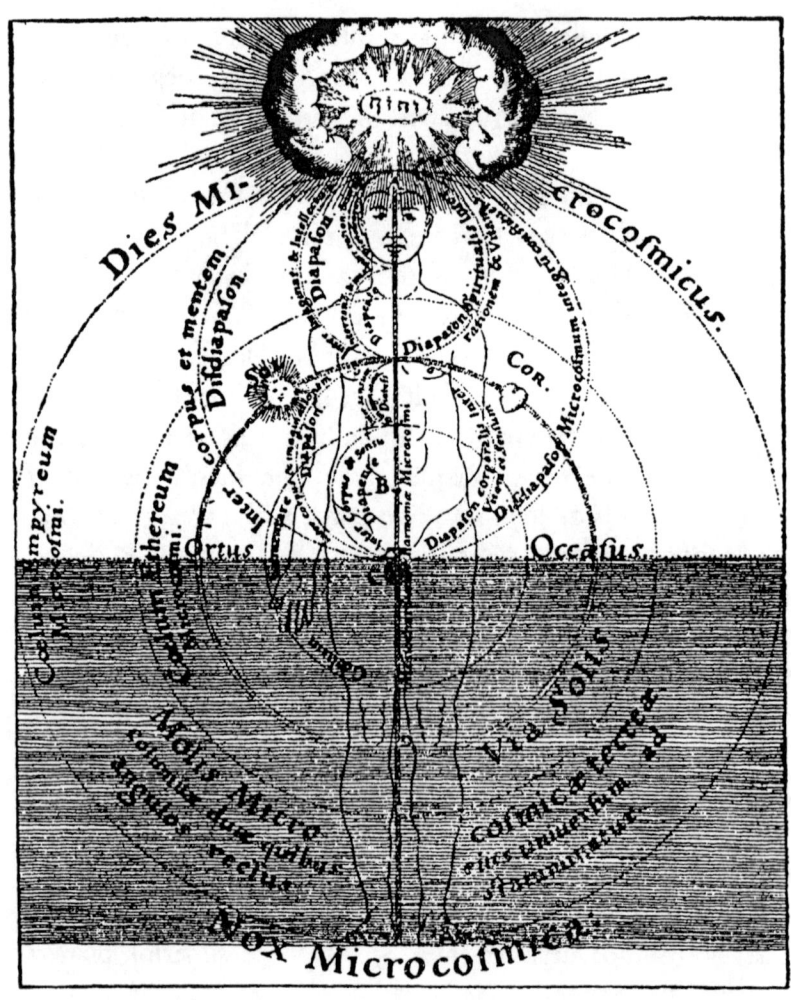

—From Collectio Operum.

THE HARMONIC INTERVALS OF THE HUMAN BODY.

represent the low mountain or hill upon which stood the holy temple—the heart. Below the ethereal heaven and separated again by a double line are the spheres of the elements—the sublunary world, the land of darkness and death, marked A,

B, C, and D in the diagram. In the occult anatomy of man this area is the true Inferno, the home of the beast of Babylon, the throne of Mammon, the temple of Beelzebub, and all the other infernal furies. At the base of the human spine burns the so-called infernal fire, and here, in the practice of black magic, the Witches' Sabbath is celebrated. In the *Coelum Elementarium* as depicted by Fludd, fire (A), the first of the element,s is associated with the bile of the liver and the contents of the gall bladder; air (B), the second of the elements, with the blood of the liver and blood vessels; water (C), the third of the elements, with the rheum or phlegm of the abdominal cavity; and earth (D), the fourth of the elements, with the waste or refuse of the "ignoble" abdominal viscera. The three general compartments of the diagram correspond excellently with the superior triad established by the physicians of the Dark Ages, who regarded man as a septenary composed of a triad and a quaternary. The three great cavities—cranial, thoracic, and abdominal—become the thrones of the three divine agencies, and the arms and legs the symbols of the elementary quaternary. In this system was perpetuated the doctrines of the Egyptians, who maintained that man consisted primarily of a triangle and a square.

In Fludd's second figure we have a full length human being surrounded by concentric circles, with the upper part, which constitutes the torso, further broken up by the arcs and circles of the harmonic intervals with which Fludd was deeply concerned. The largest of the circles surrounding the human form and including all others within it is called the *empyrean* heaven of the microcosm and represents the auric egg of man. It is divided by a horizontal line into an upper and a lower part—the day and night of the microcosm. The words *Ortus* and *Occasus* in large letters upon the horizon line signify the rising and the setting of the microcosmic sun. A cord is stretched from the feet of the man upward until its upper end is mingled with the rays of the divine glory above. In its ascent the cord passes through six spheres or planes—three in the dark half and three in the light half of the drawing. From the figure, it is evident that Fludd is attempting to portray not only the correspondence existing between man and the world, but also the harmonic structure of each, showing how, from the concordances set up in Nature, the proportions of all bodies are derived. According to one interpretation the human form represents the Greater Adam—the Heavenly Man—whose body extends over the entire interval between darkness and light, and in a more limited sense the physical body of mortal man, the latter setting forth in its parts and members a miniature of the whole world. That part of the figure above the median, or horizon line, actually represents the invisible constitution of man, for all the truly vital members of man exist only in the superphysical sphere.

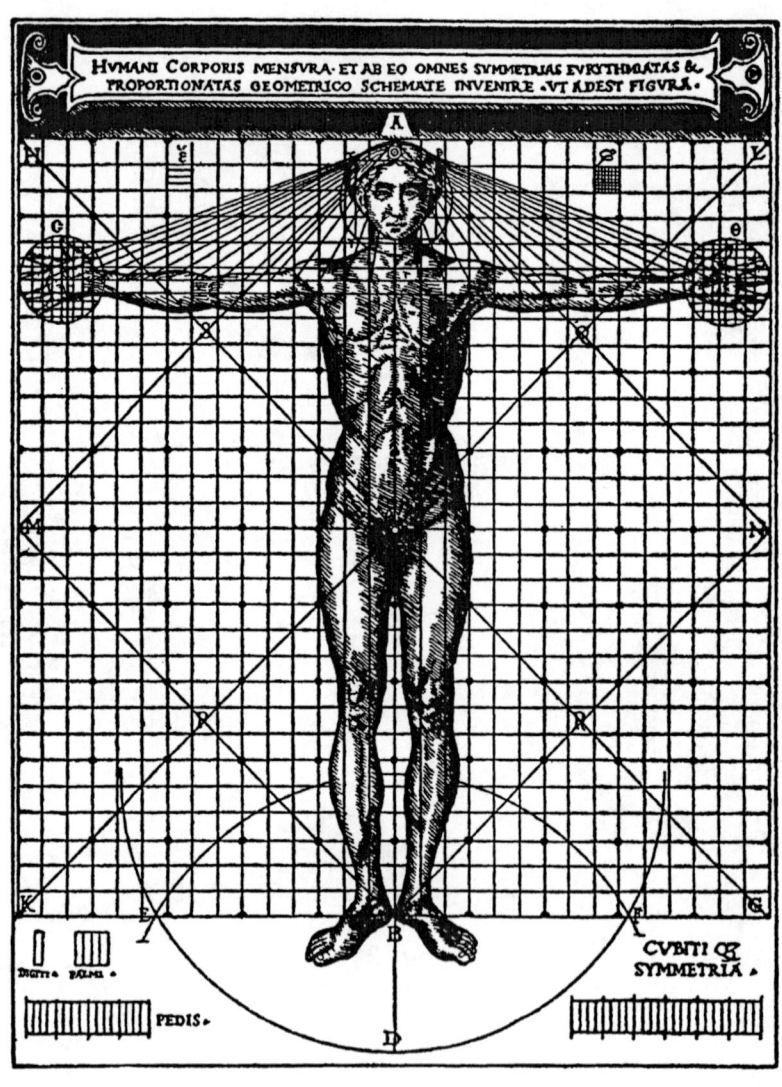

—From Cesariano's Edition of Vitruvius.

THE MACROCOSM IN ITS CREATIVE ASPECT AS FABRICATOR OF THE INFERIOR WORLD.

This is the end of this publication.

Any remaining blank pages are for our book binding requirements and are blank on purpose.

To search thousands of interesting publications like this one, please remember to visit our website at:

http://www.kessinger.net